etu
ьnev
tele

D0513829

uk

Two for Joy

Two for Joy

Scenes from Married Life

Dannie Abse

HUTCHINSON
LONDON

Published by Hutchinson 2010

2 4 6 8 10 9 7 5 3 1

First published in Great Britain in 2010 by
Hutchinson
Random House, 20 Vauxhall Bridge Road,
London SW1V 2SA

www.rbooks.co.uk

Addresses for companies within The Random House Group Limited
can be found at:
www.randomhouse.co.uk/offices.htm

The Random House Group Limited Reg. No. 954009

A CIP catalogue record for this book
is available from the British Library

ISBN 9780091931179

The Random House Group Limited supports The Forest Stewardship
Council (FSC), the leading international forest certification organisation.
All our titles that are printed on Greenpeace approved FSC certified
paper carry the FSC logo. Our paper procurement policy can be found at
www.rbooks.co.uk/environment

Mixed Sources
Product group from well-managed
forests and other controlled sources
www.fsc.org Cert no. TT-COC-2139
FSC © 1996 Forest Stewardship Council

Typeset in Bembo by Palimpsest Book Production Limited,
Grangemouth, Stirlingshire

Printed and bound in Great Britain by
CPI Mackays, Chatham ME5 8TD

For Joan again, even so.

'Nessun maggior dolore
che ricordarsi del tempo felice
nella miseria'

Inferno, V 121–3

Contents

Acknowledgements

Of the fifty poems included here, sixteen have been taken unrevised from *New and Collected Poems* (Hutchinson, 2003) along with a few new versions. A further six poems first appeared in *Running Late* (Hutchinson, 2006). All the others have been written over the last four years, some of which were recently aired in *Acumen*, *Agenda*, BBC, *London Magazine*, *Poetry Review* and *Poetry Wales*.

Author's Note

My thanks to my compatriot, the Welsh poet Tony Curtis, who first suggested I should write more scenes from married life, early and late, and so produce a companion volume to *The Presence* (Hutchinson, 2007). I'm also indebted to Siân Williams for much more than her secretarial skills and to my editor at Hutchinson, Anthony Whittome.

Two for Joy

First Meeting

Do you need second sight
to know love at first sight?

No-one gabbled on and on about fate
and the wheeling stars.

Simply, when you came near me
you trembled as aspen leaves do
and I, like Simon Magus,
thought I would levitate.

Sloppy Love Poem

'Enough amorous hyperboles,'
Catullus to his lover said.
'Let's kiss 1000 times
and after, count 1000 more.'
They untangled quickly
to undress for bed.

But one loose kiss or two
undid their duff agenda
for in their douce and moaning
dovecot they hardly knew
who was who or who was what
and forgot to count the number.

As sly deft Catullus was
so I'm dizzy-daft with you
guilty of lovers' word abuse,
wet confectionery rot: 'muse-baby',
'honey-bunny', 'sweetie-pie', 'pumpkin',
'pet', 'pudding', 'darling apricot'.

Yes, you're the world's 8th dishy
wonder and I love you, pussy cat.
Let owlish professors hoot, 'Tu-who',
it's true, it's true, it's true.
Come angel-face, ginger eyes,
juicy Joan, let's grease the pot.

The Moment

You raise your eyes from the level book
as if deeply listening. You are further than I call.
Like Eurydice you wear a hurt and absent look,
but I'm gentle for the silence into which you fall so sadly.
What are you thinking? Do you love me?
Suddenly you are not you at all but a ghost
dreaming of a castle to haunt or a heavy garden;
some place eerie, and far from me. But now a door
is banging outside, so you turn your head surprised.

You speak my name and someone else has died.

Proposal

Herschel, thrilled, observed a new star
and named it to honour a King;

Dr Livingstone found for his Queen
a waterfall, 'smoke which sounded';

and tactful Corot gave Daumier
a house 'to upset the landlord'.

What dare I promise? Mountain signposts
are few and treasures I have none.

Yet come with me, congenial, far,
up the higher indigo roads.

There, memory is imagination
and we may find an eagle's feather.

Epithalamion

Singing, today I married my white girl
beautiful in a barley field.
Green on thy finger a grass blade curled,
so with this ring I thee wed, I thee wed,
and send our love to the loveless world
of all the living and all the dead.

Now, no more than vulnerable human,
we, more than one, less than two,
are nearly ourselves in a barley field –
and only love is the rent that's due
though the bailiffs of time return anew
to all the living but not the dead.

Shipwrecked, the sun sinks down harbours
of a sky, unloads its liquid cargoes
of marigolds, and I and my white girl
lie still in the barley – who else wishes
to speak, what more can be said
by all the living against all the dead?

Come then all you wedding guests:
green ghost of trees, gold of barley,
you blackbird priests in the field,
you wind that shakes the pansy head
fluttering on a stalk like a butterfly;
come the living and come the dead.

Listen flowers, birds, winds, worlds,
tell all today that I married
more than a white girl in the barley –
for today I took to my human bed
flower and bird and wind and world,
and all the living and all the dead.

Phew!

Do you know that Sumerian proverb
'A man's wife is his destiny'?
But supposing you'd been here,
this most strange of meeting places,
5000 years too early? Or me,
a fraction of a century too late?
No angel with SF wings
would have beckoned,
'This way, madam, this way, sir.'

Have you ever, at a beach,
aimed one small pebble
at another, thrown high, higher?

And though what ends
happily
is never the end,
and though the secret is
there's another secret always,

because this, because that,
because on high the Blessèd
were playing ring-a-ring-o'-roses,
because millions of miles below,
during the Rasoumovsky,
the cellist, pizzicati,
played a comic, wrong note,
you looked to the right, luckily,
I looked to the left, luckily.

First Baby

No angel disguised as a beggar
in the brevity of a mirage
knocked on our front door.

The scarecrow did not speak,
the foxes of midnight did not bark.
No commotion of the wind.

No V-patterned squadron of swans
in their wedding gear flew over,
but we have a new birthday to mark.

Welcome daughter. Welcome, unconfined!
This is your homecoming.

Your little hands grope the air.
Your pupils are nuances of blue
and remnants of Nothing.
You cry and suddenly the world is old.

A shadow bends over you,
a silhouette hugs you close.

It's party time.
Bring in the excellent dancers.
With a hey and a ho
pipe on those oaten straws.

It was you, baby, that was crowned.
Now your mother is.
Modest, she's never seemed so proud,
proud as a chandelier and as dazzling.

More flute players are coming over the hill,
more corybantic dancers.
Bring in the flowers like compliments.
It's her royal right.

She's a benign victorious empress
and we her awe-struck servants.
Her bed's a burnished throne,
your cot's her jewel box.

What's new, baby? Everything.

Verses at Night

Britain is to get a new air raid system . . . Priority will be to estimate which direction radioactive clouds will take. This will give farmers a chance to move livestock indoors and others to stock up food.

General Sir Sidney Kirkman,
Chief of Civil Defence
17th January 1956

Sleepless, by the windowpane I stare.
   Unseen aeroplanes disturb the air.
   The ticking moon glares down aghast.
     The seven branched tree is bare.

Could this be like Hiroshima's gruesome Past,
   each fly-skinned man to raw meat cursed,
   glow of the radioactive worm,
     this, our future of the Blast?

Unreal? East and West fat Neros yearn
   for other fiddled Romes to burn;
   and so dogma cancels dogma
     and heretics in their turn.

By my wife now, I lie quiet as a
   thought of how moon and stars might blur,
   and miles of smoke squirm overhead
     rising to Man's arbiter;

the grey skins shrivelling from the head,
　our two skulls in the double bed,
　leukaemia in the soul of all,
　　flowing through the blood instead.

'No,' I cry as by her side I sprawl.
　'No,' impotently, as I hear my small
　dear daughter whimper in her cot
　　and across the darkness call.

Who?

I'm looking at my own foot. It's queer!
I peer at it with greenhorn concentration.
Thus magnified, what incongruous toenails.
Like the tree outside I pass every day
it grows ever stranger the more I stare
at it, the more I become one with it.
Again utterly odd my doctor colleague
whom I see weekdays. Just the way he walks.
What a peculiar, indolent, improper
manner of walking, come to think of it.

Or here at home, the woman I love fondly,
seemingly known – who loves me, I think.
Look! She's reading a book quite unaware;
touches her forehead, checks her cheek, cheekbone,
tip of her lovely nose, her martial lips,
her face. As if to make sure it's still there.

I wait. I stare. She raises her head puzzled
and dares to speak my name familiarly.

Photograph and White Tulips

A little nearer please. And a little nearer
we move to the window, to the polished table.
Objects become professional: mannequins
preening themselves before an audience. Only
the tulips, self-absorbed, ignore the camera.

All photographs flatter us if we wait
long enough. So we awkwardly Smile please
while long-necked tulips, sinuous out of the vase,
droop over the polished table. They're entranced
by their own puffed and smudgy reflections.

Hold it! Click. Once more! And we smile again
at one who'll be irrevocably absent.
Quick. Be quick! the tulips, like swans, will dip
their heads deep into the polished table
frightening us. Thank you. And we turn thinking,

What a fuss! Yet decades later, dice thrown,
we'll hold it, thank you, this fable of gone
youth (was that us?) and we shall smile please
and come a little nearer to the impetuous
once-upon-a-time that can never be twice.

(Never never be twice!) Yet we'll always recall
how white tulips, quick quick, changed into swans
enthralled, drinking from a polished table.
As for those white petals, they'll never fall
in that little black coffin now carrying us.

A Night Out

Friends recommended the new Polish film
at the Academy in Oxford Street.
So we joined the ever melancholy queue
of cinemas. A wind blew faint suggestions
of rain towards us, and an accordion.
Later, uneasy, in the velvet dark
we peered through the cut-out oblong window
at the spotlit drama of our nightmares:
images of Auschwitz almost authentic,
the human obscenity in close-up.
Certainly we could imagine the stench.

Resenting it, we forgot the barbed wire
was but a prop and could not scratch an eye;
those striped victims merely actors like us.
We saw the Camp orchestra assembled,
we heard the solemn gaiety of Bach,
scored by the loud arrival of an engine,
its impotent cry and its guttural trucks.
We watched, as we munched milk chocolate,
trustful children, no older than our own,
strolling into the chambers without fuss,
while smoke, black and curly, oozed from chimneys.

Afterwards, at a loss, we sipped coffee
in a bored espresso bar nearby
saying very little. You took off one glove.
Then to the comfortable suburb swiftly
where, arriving home, we garaged the car.
We asked the au pair girl from Germany
if anyone had phoned at all, or called,
and, of course, if the children had woken.
Reassured, together we climbed the stairs,
undressed together, and naked together,
in the dark, in the marital bed, made love.

A Doctor's Love Song

Since I'm heliotropic you must be my sun.
7 times by 7 times I fall at your feet.
You sulk, you smile, you're bitter-sweet.
I'm enthralled. Love, am I a fool of love?

When you're faraway I'm cold,
when you're near I almost scald.
Cynics reckon love's an illness.
Do I need a linctus?
Should I swallow bromides or a tonic?

Love's clown rules the world
not least the tides of marriage.
Listen to my heartbeat. Mitral-like it murmurs
and your cognomen is called.

I've all the signs and symptoms:
pyrexia of well-known origin,
bed-talk intimate and moronic,
loss of commonsense and blithely
certain my ailment's chronic.

Phew! Such hormonal alchemy
I feel so swimmingly alive.
Such side-effects, why panic?
I sway, I foam, I fizz,
like the top of the wave it is.
I breast-stroke and I dive.

Happily I'm legless, breathless, helpless,
and know no remedy to prescribe
till Death himself, marble-eyed,
comes home again to Arcady.

A Note Left on the Mantelpiece

(For his wife)

Attracted by their winning names I chose
Little Yid and *Welsh Bard*; years later backed
the swanky jockeys, and still thought I lacked
inspiration, the uncommon touch, not
mere expertise. Each way, I paid in prose.

Always the colours and stadiums beckoned
till, on the nose, at Goodwood, the high gods
jinxed the favourite despite the odds.
Addict that I was, live fool and dead cert.
His velvet nostrils lagged a useless second.

A poet should have studied style not form
(sweet, I regret the scarcity of roses)
but by Moses and by the nine Muses
I'll no more. Each cruising nag is a beast
so other shirts can keep the centaur warm.

Adieu, you fading furlongs of boozing,
hoarse voices at Brighton, white rails, green course.
Conclusion? Why, not only the damned horse
but whom it's running against matters.
By the way, apologies for losing.

Flowers

For my wife white freesias.
Mid-day, in a vase, their shadows flew
   to the serenity of a blank wall
when the fitful sun barged in, came through.

To my doubting father,
the hymns of bluebells, companionable.
   What greater silences than these?
Nothing better could be his tutor.

To my pious mother,
blithe daffodils from beneath the trees,
   emblems of sighing Spring. What else
could I do? Bitter, she was dying.

For my elder daughter,
a fortune-telling chain of daisies.
   Demure flirts, unbuttoned and bold,
so fresh with the dew of the garden.

For my younger daughter,
a buttercup with its golden ray
   turned on, to hold beneath the chin.
What good husband will give her butter?

For my little son enthralled,
Time's zany token of renascence
   and decay – a dandelion clock
to puff at, puff at, and blow it all away.

Sons

Sarcastic sons slam front doors.
So a far door slams and I think
of Cardiff outskirts where, once, captured acres played
at being small tamed gardens: the concrete way
roads supplanted grass, wild flowers, bosky paths.
Now my son is like that, altering every day.

I was like that; also like
those new semis that seemed ashamed,
their naked windows slashed across by whitewash.
At the frontier of Nowhere order and chaos clash.
And who's not lived at the frontier of Nowhere
and being adolescent was both prim and brash?

Strange a London door should slam
and I think thus, of Cardiff evenings
trying to rain, of quick dark where raw brick could hide,
could dream of being ruins where ghosts abide.
Do spreading lamps assert themselves too early?
Anglo-Welsh home town, half town, half countryside.

Son, you are like that and I
love you for it. In adult rooms
the hesitant sense of not belonging quite.
Too soon maturity will civilize your night,
thrust fake electric roots, the nameless becoming
consolingly named and your savage darkness bright.

Imitations

In this house, in this afternoon room,
my son and I. The other side of glass
snowflakes whitewash the shed roof and the grass
this surprised April. My son is 16,
an approximate man. He is my chameleon,
my soft diamond, my deciduous evergreen.

Eyes half closed, he listens to pop forgeries
of music – how hard it is to know – and perhaps
dreams of some school Juliet I don't know.
Meanwhile, beyond the bending window,
gusting suddenly, despite a sky half blue,
a blur of white blossom, whiter snow.

And I stare, oh immortal springtime, till
I'm elsewhere and the age my cool son is,
my father alive again (I, his duplicate),
his high breath, my low breath, sticking to the glass
while two white butterflies stumble, held each
to each, as if by elastic, and pass.

Anniversary

(At Primrose Hill, London)

The tree grows down from a bird.
The strong grass pulls up the earth
to a hill. Wade here, my dear,
through green shallows of daisies.
I hear the voice talking that is dead
behind the voice that is talking now.
The clocks of the smoky town
strike a quiet, grating sound.
Tomorrow will be the same.
Two sit on this hill and count
two moving from the two that stayed.

What happens to a flame blown out?
What perishes? Not this view,
nor my magnified hand in yours
whatever hurt and angers done.
I breathe in air the dead breathed out.
When first you inclined your face
to mine, my sweet ally came,
with your brown eyes purely wide.
My right hand on your left breast
I said, I have little to tell my dear.
For the pure bird, a pure cage.

Oh the silence that you lost
blind in the pandemonium
of the kiss and ruined was.
My dear, my dear, what perishes?
I hear this voice in a voice to come.

A Touch of Snow

Now that the evening cold is on the crocus
do you feel the ache of something missing?
Snow melts falling, a million small lights fuse

on twigs, fall to pools of darkness on the ground
while, indoors, one note's gone from the piano
– the highest. Listen to the thud of felt.

No, dear, no! Hear rather the other notes
of the right hand. Also the left background.
Their rejoicing, lamenting, candid sound.

The Cure

I feel melancholy, daughter of Lancashire.
Our neighbour has prescribed religion!
'It's your birthright and your birthmark.'
But the beautiful rod of Aaron
first with its blossom
then with its ripe almonds
is out of season.
The two drab tablets of stone
are but two drab tablets of stone
and even the Song of Solomon
on psaltery and dulcimer seems winsome.

The sun was working the shadows
in the West when Jubal saw a youth
staring at a wall, mute, depressed.
The musician plucked his octochord,
sang, 'Lift thine eyes toward the hills,
help cometh from the Lord.' In vain.
But, by chance, a certain girl strolled by
who knew the brooding boy.
She kissed him, he kissed her.
Whoops a lily, the boy began to dance.
Beloved, come this way. I, too, prefer to dance.

Saul in his tent heard David's harp
doctor away his melancholy.
It's only your voice I need to hear.
I'm cold. Stay close to me, beloved.
'Our bed is green, our rafters fir.'
Stay closer to me, beloved,
whisper code-words in my ear.
Though corn be spoilt and grapes be sharp
let your playful lashes butterfly
my irreligious cheek
and I shall kiss your birthmark.

White Balloon

Dear love, Auschwitz made me
more of a Jew than Moses did.
But the world's not always with us.
Happiness enters here again tonight
like an unexpected guest
with no memory of the future either;

enters with such an italic emphasis,
jubilant, announcing triumphantly
Hey presto and here I am and opening
the June door into our night living room
where, under the lampshade's ciliate,
an armchair's occupied by a white balloon.
As if there'd been a party.

Of course, Happiness, uninhibited,
will pick it up, his stroking thumb
squeaking a little as he leads us to the hall.
And we shall follow him, too,
when he climbs the lit staircase
towards the landing's darkness,
bouncing bouncing the white balloon
from hand to hand.

It's bedtime; soon we must dream
separately – but what does it matter now
as the white balloon is thrown up high?
Quiet, so quiet, the moon above Masada
and closed, abandoned for the night,
the icecream van at Auschwitz.

Ants

What would be left of our tragedies if a literate insect were to present us his?

Cioran

My gentle wife, convinced pacifist, finds
all ants loathsome. When on crawling duty
for their Queen they remind her of armies
carrying home their carrion booty.

So, imperturbably, my wife, anti-ant,
stamps on them mercilessly. Some become blurs;
but she can't annihilate all those moving
columns of black-uniformed scavengers.

Down and down her thudding foot bombs
the wingless neuters. They must shed calories
as, desperate, they flee and excavate
safe Maginot trenches, darker galleries.

Now my wife (sweet to kiss) pours boiling water
over them. Most die noiselessly for their Queen
as my darling floods the kitchen floor, napalms
the step to Dis outside the door with steam.

Still surviving ants panic and scurry
but will soon regroup as if commanded, return
like hoodwinked soldiers to the battlefield
for the Queen's employment. They'll bleed and burn.

Domestic, 3 a.m.

Where the apple reddens
Never pry
Lest we lose our Edens
Eve and I.
Robert Browning

You need not be cross, why are you
cross-examining me?

By Ishara, queen of the oaths,
hear me out.
       – Let's contend no more love –

By Ishtar of Nineveh,
by Ishtar of Hatterina
       – do not shout;
what so wild as words are? –

By the fat hypertensive lord of wars,
by St Francis's cat and Santa Claus,
by Gog and Magog and Eskimo Nell,
I, on quitting the flat of Mel and Priscilla,
was caught in the cage of a bloody lift
rattling its bars like a bloody gorilla
and ringing the bloody emergency bell.

I could have been there till Hogmanay.
       – Stop staring at me like that.

By the black pigeons of Dodena,
I could have been there till doomsday –

Please

I'll hoist the white flag high,
I'll blow the bugle of retreat,
I'm already on my knees,
I'll fall 7 times before your feet.
What else, my darling, can I say
except I'm starving and I love you?
OK . . . OK?

Thankyou Note

for the unbidden swish of morning curtains
you opened wide – letting sleep-baiting shafts
of sunlight enter to lie down by my side;
for adagio afternoons when you did the punting
(my toiling eyes researched the shifting miles of sky);
for back-garden evenings when you chopped the wood
and I, incomparably, did the grunting;
(a man too good for this world of snarling
is no good for his wife – truth's the safest lie);

for applauding my poetry, O most perceptive spouse;
for the improbable and lunatic, my darling;
for amorous amnesties after rancorous rows
like the sweet-nothing whisperings of a leafy park
after the blatant noise of a city street
(exit booming cannons, enter peaceful ploughs);
for kindnesses the blind side of my night-moods;
for lamps you brought in to devour the dark.

Condensation on a Windowpane

1

I want to write something simple,
something simple, few adjectives,
ambiguities disallowed.

Something old-fashioned:
a story of Time perhaps
or, more daringly, of love.

I want to write something simple
that everyone can understand,
something simple as pure water.

But pure water
is H_2O
and that's complicated
like steam, like ice, like clouds.

2

My finger squeaks on glass.
I write JOAN
I write DANNIE.
Imagine! I'm a love-struck
youth again.

I want to say something
without ambiguity.
Imagine! me, old-age pensioner
wants to say something
to do with love and Time,
love that's simple as water.

But long ago we learnt
water is complicated,
is H_2O, is ice, is steam, is cloud.

Our names on the window
begin to fade.
Slowly, slowly.
They weep as they vanish.

An Interrupted Letter

In this room's winterlight the travail of
a letter to a new widow. Solemn,
the increasing enterprise of age.
I stutter. Consoling words come slow,
seem false, as if spoken on a stage.
It would be easier to send flowers.

I think of her closing her husband's eyelids
and I look up. Siberian snow hesitated,
then parachuted into our garden
for hours, confiscating yesterday's
footprints. Shall I send flowers?

But now my wife, unaware in the far kitchen,
suddenly sings, captivating me,
my pen mid-air above a muffled page.

When we were young, tremulant with Spring,
often off-key she'd sing her repertoire –
dateless folk songs, dance tunes dated.
In her Pears-suds bath I'd hear her,
in the Morris Minor with our kids.

I must return to my hiemal letter.
Sing on love, as once you did, sing and sing
for past youth, for hungers unabated.

Last Words

Splendidly, Shakespeare's heroes,
Shakespeare's heroines, once the spotlight's on,
enact every night, with such grace, their verbose deaths.
Then great plush curtains, then smiling resurrection
to applause – and never their good looks gone.

The last recorded words too
of real kings, real queens, all the famous dead,
are but pithy pretences, quotable fictions
composed by anonymous men decades later,
never with ready notebooks at the bed.

Most do not know who they are
when they die or where they are, country or town,
nor which hand on their brow. Some clapped-out actor may
imagine distant clapping, bow, but no real queen
will sigh, 'Give me my robe, put on my crown.'

Death scenes not life-enhancing,
death scenes not beautiful nor with breeding;
yet bravo Sydney Carton, bravo Duc de Chavost
who, euphoric beside the guillotine, turned down
the corner of the page he was reading.

And how would I wish to go?
Not as in opera – that would offend –
nor like a blue-eyed cowboy shot and short of words,
but finger-tapping still our private morse, '. . . love you,'
before the last flowers and flies descend.

New Granddaughter

You don't know the score, what's you, what's not.
Remote ancestors return you can't disown.
This prelude, this waiting for an encore.

Is that raised hand yours, this wind-pecked morning?
Enigmatic trees, askew, shake above the pram.
All's perplexity, green reverie, shadowland.

But why this grandfatherly spurt of love?
Your skin is silk, your eyes suggest they're blue.
I bend to smell small apricots and milk.

Did I dream that legend of the Angel
who falls to touch each baby's fontanelle
and wipe out racial memory, leaving *déjà vu*?

I'm confessing! Your newness, petite, portends
my mortality – a rattle for you, the bell for me.
Hell, I'm old enough to mutter blessings.

The determinates of the clock increase.
Sometimes you close your eyes noiselessly, turn
your head, listening to music that has ceased.

Inscription on the Flyleaf
of a Bible

(For Larne)

Doubting, read what this fabled history teaches,
how the firework, Imagination, reaches high
to dignify and sanctify.

You need not, granddaughter, be religious
to learn what Judges, Kings, Prophets, yield,
thought-lanterns for Life's darker field,
moral lies of piety and poetry.

You need not, granddaughter, hosanna heroes:
this wily shepherd, that bloodthirsty tough;
yet applaud the bulrush child
who, when offered gold, chose the coal.
Satisfied, the tyrant Pharaoh smiled,
did not see the pattern in the whole.

Forgive the triumphalism and the pride,
forego the curses and the ritual stuff.
You, older, I hope, will always side
with the enslaved and hunted,
deride the loud and lethal crowd
who vilify and simplify.

What is poetry but the first words
Adam, amazed, spoke to Eve?
On the first page of Genesis
hear the next to Nothing.
Later sound-effects, God off-stage, or theurgic stunts,
(water from a rock, a bush ablaze) might deceive
but bring ladders only to nerveless heaven.
Better to walk with Jephthah's luckless daughter
among real hills. And grieve.

Enjoy David's winging gifts to praise;
Solomon's rapturous serenade; also Job's
night-starred elegance of distress –
though such eloquence can bless,
indiscriminately, the last flags of the just
and the unjust on the barricade.

Read, granddaughter, these scandalous stories,
screaming Joseph in the pit of scorpions,
champion Goliath of course outclassed;
so many cubits of sorrow and delight,
so many visions of our ruffian Past.
They do not stale or fade
and may fortify and mollify.

A Marriage

Love, almost three score licit years have passed
(racist fools said our marriage would not last)
since our student days, honeysuckle nights,
when you'd open the jammed sashed window
above the dark basement flat and I, below,
would be an urgent, athletic Romeo.

Remember when I hacked my shin and swore
and you put an exclamation mark to your lips
because of the German landlady's law
NO VISITORS AFTER 10 P.M.
She kept castrating instruments for men!

Up the creaking stairs Indian file, the door
closed, you'd play before one amorous word
a Louis Armstrong record or another diverting disc
lest something of our nothings would be heard.

Oh the stealth of my burglar's exit through the dark,
the landlady's dog that we called Wagner
alert, anti-Semitic, lifting its ears
to rehearse a virtuoso chilling bark.

I hear its echo still at the front garden gate,
down the lamplit street, faint, through the hurrying years
to where we are, in sickness and in health,
in perdurable love, ageing together,
lagging somewhat, slowly running late.

The Malham Bird

That long summer a clarity of marvels
yet no morning News announced the great world
had been reinvented and we were new,
in love – you a Gentile and I a Jew!

Dear wife, remember our first illicit
holiday, the rented room, the hidden beach
in Wales, the tame seagull that seemed a portent,
a love message, as if Dafydd's ghost had sent it?

After our swim we lay on our shadows naked,
more than together, and saw high in the blue
two chalk lines kiss and slowly disappear.
Then the friendly gull swooped down, magnified, near.

Now, three grandchildren later, I think of
a black feathered bird, the malham of Eden,
how it took advice, closed its eyes resolute,
when others singing pecked forbidden fruit;

and how, of all the birds, it was not banished
but stayed, lonely, immortal, forever winging
over the vanished gardens of Paradise.

In My Fashion

Dear, they said that woman resembled you.
Was that why I went with her, flirted with her,
raised my right hand to her left breast
till I heard the still sad music of humanity?
I complimented you! Why do you object?

Still you shrill, discover everything untrue:
your doppelgänger does not own your birthmarks,
cannot know our blurred nights together.
That music was cheap – a tune on a comb at best,
harsh and grating. Yes, you chasten me

and subdue. Well, that woman was contraband
and compared with you mere counterfeit.
Snow on the apple tree is not apple blossom –
all her colours wrong, approximate,
as in a reproduction of a masterpiece.

A Scene from Married Life

That unseasonable July in Ogmore
nothing was happening until it happened,
the commuters trapped in their stuffy office block,
the sea slow, the Monday beach sullen, empty,

and I, thinking of the squabble with my wife:
fast barbed words that made the other squirm
and fed flushed indignation, verbal revenge –
a dead bird eaten by the early worm.

I piled up my usual clothes and daps tidily
on a convenient boulder brooding nearby
and, troubled, saw the far dank confusion of
the sea and sky in resentful wedlock.

A mile out the monstrous Tusker Rock crammed
with ghosts and psychopomps raised black fangs.
So many boats it had torn asunder. Seagulls
drifted above it like lost thoughts of the damned.

Soon, daring the fussy sea, I entered
a B movie to enact my great climactic scene.
(After I sank – weep for me – the credits would come up,
then the screen, appropriately, would go blank.)

I swivelled for a last winsome longshot, saw
on the high cliff my wife dressed in blue and all
the best of the world true and desirable.
With surrendering waves I crawled to the shore.

Our own cold wars during the real Cold War
were few and brief. Sulky, I'd linger at my desk
but children's cries were mightier than the pen.
And sweet the armistice, each kiss, and then . . .

Yesterday's Tiff

You were ready to boil at 0°.
I wasn't sulking. Simply I thought
no more figs and honey for you,

no more ginger to match your eyes.
Exit Poussin. 'Bye Kandinsky.
Through the window, wham!

You like rum. Down the drain with it.
Raspberries? I've eaten them all.
Go to bed with Ruskin!

That dinner party you plan.
I'll invite Kingsley
and other right-wing boring guests.

A war-monger or two. Do you get
the drift of what I'm saying?
Definitely no more freesias.

Only things that keep you awake
at night: shuffling mice, coffee,
and now, please, me too, silly.

The Runners

Past a buckthorn shrub
which had captured
a blue plastic bag,
up the high sandhills
of mid-day, mid-week Ogmore,
we lifted our heavy feet
as if we suffered
a sudden ataxia.

Everywhere, silences,
pathless directions.
We climbed further to see
the way down. You said,
'Like the ergs of the Sahara.'
I stared at the bird-loved
yellow berries of a shrub
turning into Nubian gold.

Then, descending single file,
5 runners appeared.
White shorts, white vests.
From nowhere. Towards us.
On the deaf sand, weary-faced,
one of terrible aspect
so close we heard
their intimate breathing.

In an instant
they had vanished
like light in an empty room
when a cloud passes over,
leaving us wide-awake,
hearts beating together
in the astonishment
of the real.

Two for Joy

Still as near and as distant as a hyphen
the way it was, it could have been our first tryst
that flat Sunday afternoon serious as a vow.
(The other faces in the tranquil carriage
inscrutably bored by the train's pitapat.)
And we so long together, you so long adored,
still in our leaping time did not desist
what the old grammar of love would allow
in public – and wouldn't have done even that
had we not seen, at the outskirts of the town,
a single magpie, dressed to kill, float down
where insistent vanishings of smoke arose
from the slowly receding allotments.
Thoughtfully we turned to each other and kissed.

With Compliments

Dear, if I had a small legacy from Croesus
I would purchase – please do not argue –
that painting of gladioli by Soutine
you so admired. But in a waking fit
of realism I've bought
this bunch of robust-red,
radiantly alive upstanding gladioli
from The Corner Flower Stall instead.

Just a Moment

As my wife arranges the lilac in a vase
I think how for years I've stared from this window
at that garden tree so stark it seemed ashamed;
or as now in May, proud – dressed to the nines,
rustling its green silks and in stately bloom.

I've stood here observing Time's sorcery,
the petroleum sunset behind its branches,
the midges energetic above the grass,
or the rising moon a phoenix in its high leaves.

I have grown old watching such things
and thought how a poet's late adagios
like those of Beethoven (*Muss es sein?*)
should say more about the seasons of fate
than the years have wings and the hours pass.

But now I'm attentive to the window itself
and, for a moment, I've cracked it again, trespassed
into the half-mad timeless world that is still
where I am not old nor will be older –
the tip of my tongue against the glass,
the chill touch of it, the nothing taste of it,
until I breathe in the jubilant Yes
and mortally precarious fragrance of lilac
my wife has just placed upon the windowsill.

Lachrymae

(i)   The Accident

I crawled from the noise of the upturned car
and the silence in the dark began to grow.
I called out her name again and again
to where neither words nor love could go.

(ii)   Later

I went to her funeral.
I cried.
I went home that was not home.

What happened cannot keep.
Already there's a perceptible change of light.
Put out that light. Shades
lengthen in the losing sun.
She is everywhere and nowhere
now that I am less than one.

Most days leave no visiting cards behind
and still consoling letters make me weep.
I must wait for pigeon memory
to fly away, come back changed
to inhabit aching somnolence
and disguising sleep.

(iii)   Winter

What is more intimate
than a lover's demure whisper?
Like the moment before Klimt's *The Kiss*.
What more conspiratorial
than two people in love?

So it was all our eager summers
but now the yellow leaf has fallen
and the old rooted happiness
plucked out. Must I rejoice when
teardrops on a wire turn to ice?

Last night, lying in bed,
I remembered how, pensioners both,
before sleep, winter come,
your warm foot suddenly
would console my cold one.

(iv)   Swan Song

Night fuzzy fairground music
and, like kids, we sat astride
daft horses bouncing on
the lit-wide Merry-Go-Round
to swagger away, serene,
old lovers hand in hand.

Now, solemn, I watch
the spellbound moon again,
its unfocused clone drowned
in Hampstead's rush-dark pond
where a lone swan sings
without a sound.

Postcard to His Wife

Wish you were here. It's a calm summer's day
and the dulcamara of memory
is not enough. I confess without you
I know the impoverishment of self
and the Venus de Milo is only stone

So come home. The bed's too big! Make excuses.
Hint we are agents in an obscure drama
and must go North to climb 2000 feet
up the cliffs of Craig y Llyn to read
some cryptic message on the face of a rock.

Anything! But come home. Then we'll motor,
just you, just me, through the dominion
of Silurian cornfields, follow the whim
of twisting narrow lanes where hedges
have wild business with roses and clematis.

Or we could saunter to the hunkered blonde
sanddunes and, blessed, mimic the old gods
who enacted the happy way to be holy.
Meanwhile, dear, your husband is so uxorious
absence can't make Abse's heart grow fonder.

Now and Then

(After Pushkin)

As the drooping autumn flowers touch us
more than those that bloom in spring
so the plaintive mood returns to when
                              we parted
more than the candy minutes when
                              we courted
and timelessness was everything.

After the Memorial

Some spoke of her unostentatious beauty:
she, passionate moralist, Truth's sweet secretary.
No-one heard the sobbing of the angels.

Well, I have my own weeping to do.
(If angels could weep they would become human.)
I lived her life and she lived mine –
not only in the easy valleys of Pretend
where bosky paths descend to lakes where no swan
is singular (and fish ignore the hunched Angler)

but here where the uphill road to happiness
has ordinary speed limits,
and still the revelation is
that there can be such a thing

until it must yield to a dead end.

So now our marriage book is drowned
(there seemed magic in it)
and she is both manifest and concealed –
manifest because I see her everywhere,
concealed because she is nowhere to be found.

Portrait of an Old Poet

(To Graham Kershaw)

Does the future slyly haunt all portraits,
a preternatural unveiling? It's as if
you saw me, a man grieving who would know
his dear one turned to stone on the M4.

For you caught me there sitting downcast
with arms folded, commanded to do so
by some strange authority – the white
balloon of happiness out of sight.

Sometimes children mime gargoyle-grim
faces in the mirror. The old don't have to!
But till that night when Death divorced us
I'd been nearly as happy as possible.

So I wish you'd painted in the white balloon
we chased after, that I'd pursue still
though it floats up far, smaller and smaller
into the blue and once upon a time.

The Revisit

This scene too beautiful, it seemed a fake:
the sunset sky, the drowning sunset lake.
With you by my side, did I dream awake?

God's spacious canvases always amaze
even when lucid colours become uncertain greys.
There was nothing else we could do but praise.

Yet darkness, like dread, lay within the scene
and you said, 'Just like music that seems serene.'
(Mozart stared at green till he became the green.)

And there, above the lake, of course unsigned,
its surface hoofed with colour by the wind,
were great windows between clouds, fires behind,

as if from Angel wars. Such April bloodshed!
The wide sky-fires flared and their glitter-red
sparks cooled to scattered stars instead.

Now I, bereaved, like the bruised sky in disrepair,
a shadow by my side, hear a far owl's thin despair.
I stare at colour till I am the stare.

The gradual distance between two stars is night.
Ago, love, we made love till dark was bright.
Now without you dark is darker still and infinite.

Magnolia

A happening, a green place, a door slamming,
an almost empty restaurant at night,
a perfume perhaps, anything may provoke
a dormant picture at the back of the mind
to awaken and advance and remind.

So she is with me in the light and dark.

A sunbeam coming and going suddenly
in a quiet room. Always suddenly.
Musical notes from the open window
of a passing car's radio, maybe.

Each day is remembrance day, adagio,
for the new widower and widow.

Their memories, I know, all begin with We.

In the walled garden of Golders Hill Park
the names of the local unfamous dead
are inscribed on wooden benches
in defiance of the ephemeral. There, now,
among the flowers disguised as colours
in competition with each other, their queen,
a magnolia tree, rules supreme, magnificently.

Memory, father of tears, we sat beneath
it once detained by its audacious efflorescence
that's too quick and too brief. It's nature's
festive haiku, it's a magician's vanishing trick.
Hoopla! First you see it, then it's been!

In serene marital silence we observed
its bridal branches slowly violated,
insolently shamed by a small pilfering wind –
white blossom drifting down as in a dream
without a sound, a trifle blood-stained.

Later, we spoke of transience and of Pierre
Magnol, French botanist of the 17th century,
and how magnolias are named after him
though he's long forgotten, his life wiped clean.

On Parole

Dear, so much shared. Then suddenly, solitary
confinement with the cell door half open,
sentence indefinite. After two years I dared.

You would not have liked or disliked her.
By day her sunlight lively and warming.
At night no lighthouse signalled sweet danger

and I on parole from the prison of mourning
where remembrances recur like a circle
till everything's a blur – every damn thing

a tear-blur, for we'd been utterly darned
together: knew light's secret delight: colour.
You gave me all the light you were

so to embrace another seemed a betrayal.
Not so. How could it be? But next morning
her gold was still gold – my silver, pale tinsel.

Stale, dressed in black again, I blinked at the green,
daunting, unsafe world that indisputably is,
then yours faithfully slouched back to jail.

The Violin Player

Too often now, half somnolent, I would go
like Yeats to a fortunate Lake Isle where
unblemished water-lilies never die,
and no solitary swan floats by
from everlasting to everlasting.

And in the tranquil orchard of this Isle
I'd plunder such paradisial apples
that Cezanne could have painted – apples
no bird would have dared to peck at,
fraudulent but beautiful.

Yes, I would go there rapt, recreant,
and stay there because, sweet, you're not here
till, self-scolded, I would recollect
my scruffy, odorous Uncle Isidore
(surely one of the elect) who played

unsettling, attenuated music
long after a string had snapped,
whose beard bent down to interject,
'Little boy, who needs all the lyric strings?
Is the great world perfect?'

Letters

During an unimportant afternoon,
while an appropriate fuss of rain
patters tearfully on a window pane
(your ashes outside in the Ogmore garden),
I read ink-fading letters from your jammed
desk drawer; the earliest, candid and gauche,
when you were 21 and I was 24.

Then we were dunces of love-talk.
Now others, mellow, summon you to keep
the lonely robin in the garden company.
Bending and rising, bending and rising,
you pull up a serious weed or two,
wearing my patched Harris-tweed coat,
Oxfam-rejected – much too big for you.

Look! You've kept my card from Grau du Roi
where I asked for bread, received a rabbit.
You laughed, explained that I was le
and you were la. Now I read sweet words
I daren't repeat. (You would not want me to.)
In mute distress, my hand is at my throat
till I feel nothing like a scar.

I return the letters to the drawer of dust
and dark and paper-clip. They follow
the motion of our marriage, its yes, its no,
its turning axle and escorting felloe,
the 'I love you' peppered with a quip,
the fervent poetry of love-making,
the sober prose of friendship.

Like

an English summer's day?
Child at the window, lunatic
driving the home-asylum mad,
screaming Rain rain go away
come again another bloody day,
And, outside, the darling buds of May
wet, odourless. I hum Shakespeare's No!

And a No to Burns's self-admiring
red red rose – too June insolent, too
overblown, too wantonly perfumed;
rather I would have compared thee
to those shyest of flowers
that must be held so close
before their scent is known.

The Presence

Though not sensible I feel we are married still.
After four years survival guilt endures.
I should have said this, could have done that,
and your absent presence has left a weeping scar.
Like a heartbeat, you are indispensable.

Each year, I think, the cries of the dead retreat,
become smaller, small. Now your nearness is far
and sometimes I sense you're hardly there at all.
When in company, when my smiles persist,
your distance briefly is like the furthest star.

It's when I'm most myself, most alone
with all the clamour of my senses dumb,
then, in the confusion of Time's deletion
by Eternity, I welcome you and you return
improbably close, though of course you cannot come.

Postscript

Inexplicable splendour makes a man sing
as much as the pointlessness of things;

and you conceded how sweetly the wide-eyed
disfigured of the world's circus have sung
and the powdered clowns in their darkness sing.

So though late, all too late, is it demeaning
to publish love lyrics about you now?
Bitter to recall that once I pleaded,

Love, read this though it has little meaning
for by reading this you give me meaning.